Fontaine Fox's

TOONERVILLE TROLLEY

Fontaine Fox's
TOONERVILLE TROLLEY

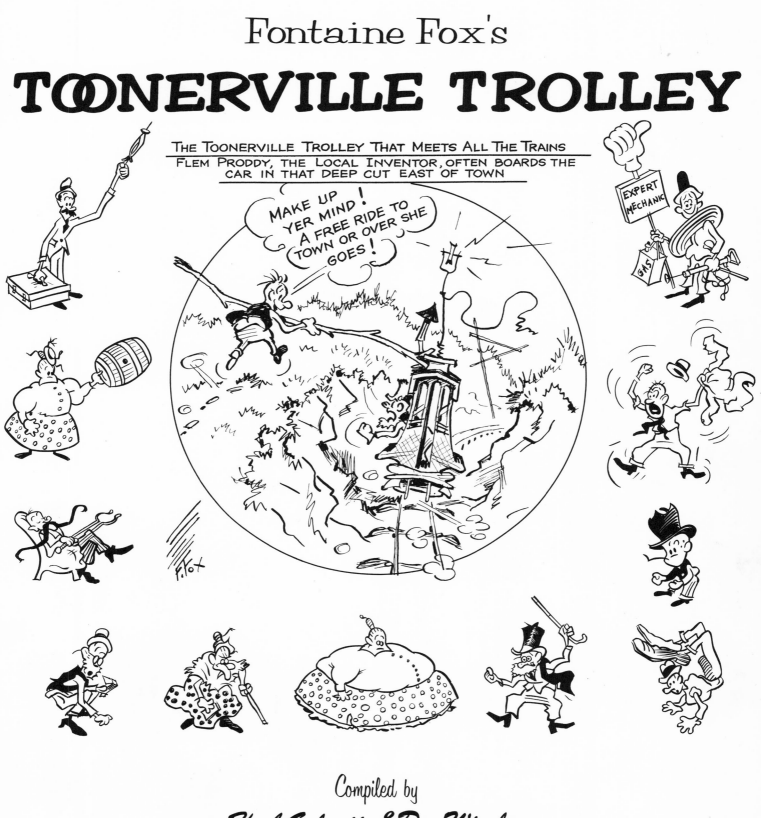

Compiled by

Herb Galewitz & Don Winslow

Charles Scribner's Sons • New York

Acknowledgment

Some of the cartoons herein were photographed from a collection held by the Lilly Library in Bloomington, Indiana. We wish to thank that organization and especially Miss Elfrieda Lang, Curator of Manuscripts, for their courtesy and help.

The balance of cartoons was assembled from those "zany, oddball" collectors who have been clipping and saving newspaper cartoons since the days of Opper and Swinnerton. With their help, the history of comic art becomes an exciting and stimulating voyage. Thank you, fellows.

Printed in the United States of America
Library of Congress Catalog Card Number 70-39325
SBN 684-12899-3 (Trade cloth)

c 1

Contents

Introduction

Remember when vacant lots abounded in our land and kids played on them the year round? Remember when trolley cars crisscrossed every street and some lines ended in the "country"? Remember tomboys, when that term was used without reference to a sexual aberration? Remember chaperones, and when elderly people were a vigorous part of the community? Remember when suburbia could be located only a few miles from downtown?

Fontaine T. Fox did and he recorded that era faithfully and humorously in his marvelous *Toonerville Folks* cartoons that ran for over forty years.

The humor highlighted the idiosyncrasies of the Toonerville populace. Their individual traits were spotlighted and brought into sharp focus in the daily gag panels. There were no John Does. Everyone had a "handle," a nickname to alert one to the humorous possibilities. You weren't just *Mr. Flint,* but rather *Banker Flint* or *Old Man Flint.* Fox, of course, didn't start this. He just continued the practice that goes back to the Middle Ages and possibly before. Nowadays, the use of nicknames is diminishing. (Don't tell me about Billy, Dick and Bobby. They don't count.) Our teachers and parents claimed that nicknames weren't nice. They were vulgar and made fun of people. The authorities were quite right, but then again, if you were just a fellow who loved to overeat, you didn't go through life as another blob, but rather as "Fat." You had your position in the order of things. It might take a while to get used to the appellation, but by then you had an identity. Isn't that worth the torment?

Fox used the "handles" as they were appropriate to the times. After all, he was giving us a look at a period of American life, and he gave it to us warts and all.

When Fox's father, a judge and editorial writer, saw his son's first published cartoon in the *Louisville Herald,* he thundered, ". . . it's a mighty queer way to make a living," and stormed out of the room much in the manner of the Terrible Tempered Mr. Bang. If he used the word "queer" in the sense of being unique, then Mr. Fox, Sr., was indeed prophetic. At the height of their popularity, the cartoons of Fontaine Fox appeared in almost three hundred newspapers, daily and Sunday. Toys, games, books, movies, and ads (Vaseline, for one) were issued featuring the singular Toonerville characters. In 1933, the black heart of the Depression, *Fortune* magazine estimated that Fox's income from newspaper syndication alone was $1,400 a week.

One famous child star tried to cash in on the popularity of Mickey (Himself) McGuire, Fox's tough Irish kid, and adopted his name for a series of films. Fox sued and actor Joe Yule, Jr., again changed his name, this time to Mickey Rooney.

That first published cartoon was political and came after two ventures into straight reporting had ended in near disaster. Fox, just out of Louisville's Boys' High School, was sent to spy on a secret nudist colony. An irate member discovered him, and with a right to the jaw sent the cub reporter fleeing. Later, he was sent to a local racetrack to sketch a local sportsman with a celebrated hooked nose. The artwork was too accurate and Fox again had to flee the swipes of the cane-wielding gentleman.

In 1904, Fox went to Indiana University and, in his second year on campus, supported himself by sending a cartoon a day to the *Louisville Herald* for $12 a week. However, he had to put the finished drawing each night on the 1:10 A.M. train to ensure its safe arrival in Kentucky. After one year of moonlighting, Fox left the university to return to Louisville as a full-time cartoonist and sketch artist for the *Times*. He also had more time to play baseball, which he had excelled in during high school and college days. Now, he joined a semi-pro team, the Dusty Rhodes, which played in the west end of Louisville. The senior Fox frowned on Sunday baseball, so young Fontaine told him that he spent the Sabbath visiting a girl who lived on a farm in Indiana. He actually did go to see the girl, but only on those days when the ballgame was rained out. The girl's farmer father was always glad to see Fox as when he came he brought the welcome rain.

After four years of sharpening his art technique on political and topical subjects, Fox accepted an offer to work on the *Chicago Post*. The king of cartoonists in Chicago at that time was John McCutcheon of the *Tribune*. He did political, topical, and general atmospheric work much in the vein of his fellow Hoosier and poet, James Whitcomb Riley.

McCutcheon was one of the first cartoonists to use children in his art and they were very popular. Therefore, when Fox approached his managing editor, Leigh Reilly, for permission to do humorous cartoons of children to break up the steady diet of political work, the reply was that McCutcheon was already doing it and how dare he [Fox] compete with the acknowledged master in his own town! Fox pointed out that McCutcheon's kids were in the Tom Sawyer country mold, while his kids would come from that new area of population growth, the suburbs.

Reilly relented and let Fox try a few. The first one showed a mother and a small boy waiting for a streetcar. (A symbol of things to come!) As the car appeared, the mother discovered that the boy had wandered into a vacant lot, where he found a derby and was trying it on. The last panel was set in a barbershop, where the boy's hair is being shampooed and his stern mother looks on. The editor liked the strip and printed it on the front page, and put Fox on a one-a-week humorous cartoon schedule.

By 1915, Fox had joined the Wheeler Syndicate and his national success was launched. He moved to New York, the headquarters for the Syndicate, and started to enlarge his stock cast of characters, which now included *Thomas Edison, Jr., Sissie,* and *Grandma, the Demon Chaperone.*

Fox, like most other cartoonists, relied on everyday events and ordinary people as source material for his gags and characters. His most famous creation was inspired by a friendly old bearded motorman who ran a rundown trolley in Pelham, New York. Fox had traveled on his line on a visit to cartoonist Charlie Voight's home. (Voight is best remembered for his comic strip *Betty.)* By the time Fox returned to his own home, he had recalled another rundown trolley line in Louisville, the Brook Street run. He merged the two lines into *The Toonerville Trolley That Meets All Trains* and its conductor-motorman, the Skipper. It was an immediate success.

Fox credited his own father as the prototype for *the Terrible Tempered Mr. Bang,* but Mrs. Fox claimed that Fox himself was the original Mr. Bang. Fox readily admitted that he used Mr. Bang as an outlet for his pet peeves. For example, Fox once went to a movie where he paid his admission. Inside he was informed by the usher that there would be a wait for seats. Fox fumed, but like most of us said nothing. But the next day he drew a cartoon of Mr. Bang in the same situation, who reacted by grabbing the usher by the seat of his pants and airborning him to the outside of the theater to make an announcement that there were no seats inside.

Mickey McGuire and *The Little Scorpions* were replicas of boyhood chums in Louisville.

The Powerful Katrinka was a combination of a black female cook who worked for Fox's father and Ole Olson, a football character out of a George Fitch novel.

For art inspiration, the young Fox turned to John Leech, the great British caricaturist. He found his illustrations in *Comic History of England* (1848) by Gilbert Abbott à Beckett. Though the styles of Leech and Fox are about as unrelated as any two artists, Fox did attribute his early knowledge of expression to a study of that book. Fox's scratchy style is deceptively simple. Though at times he had assistants to help with the backgrounds, Fox could never find anyone to draw the characters to his own satisfaction. Once Fox had the subject idea, the drawing was done quite rapidly, and at the same time he accompanied himself by singing a few stanzas of those turn-of-the-century mournful ballads, "The Baggage Coach Ahead" or "The Browns Have Lost Their Baby Boy." Luckily, the songs never pervaded the art.

Toonerville Folks reached the end of the line on February 9, 1955, when the seventy-year-old Fox retired to Florida. Wisely, neither the Syndicate nor Fox sought a replacement. The "vacant lot" era of American life was disappearing. It was beaten by the population explosion of post-World War II, suburban developers, and urban blight. Today, seventeen years later, we have "progressed" to professional Little Leagues, artificial grass, and the disappearance of street life. It is enough to make a grown man cry.

Fontaine Fox died August 9, 1964, in Greenwich, Connecticut.

Herb Galewitz

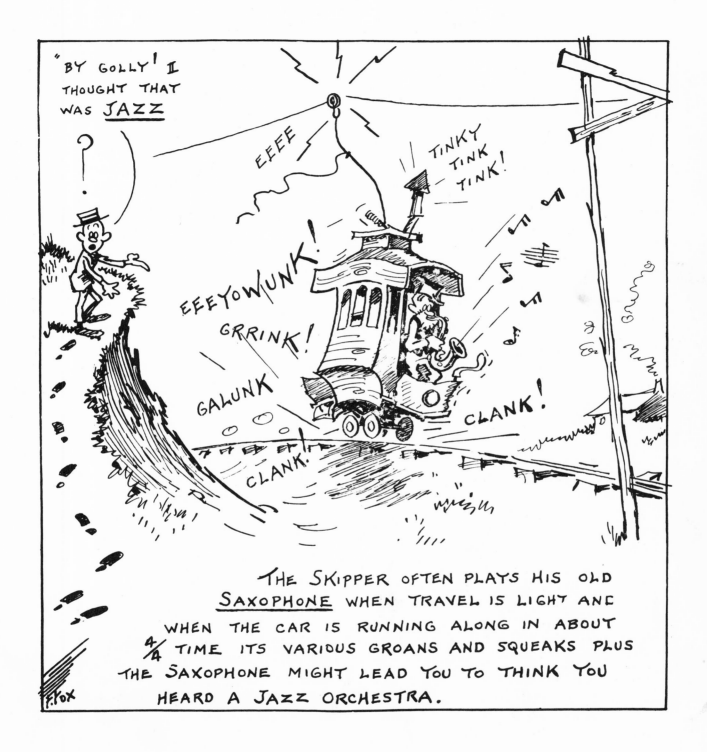

THE SKIPPER'S EYE-SIGHT SURE AIN'T WHAT IT USED TO BE!

NOBODY EVER STAYS VERY LONG IN THAT HOUSE ON KNOB HILL WHICH COMMANDS A VIEW OF THE ENTIRE LENGTH OF THE TROLLEY LINE

THE SKIPPER HAS THOSE TIN CANS ON THE POSTS SO HE CAN GAMBLE WITH UNCLE "CHEW" WILSON, 2 QUID MAN

WHEN THERE ARE NO PASSENGERS THE SKIPPER OFTEN AMUSES HIMSELF WITH A SORT OF POLO SOLITAIRE

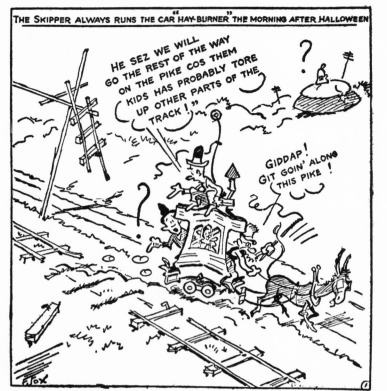

The Skipper often pockets his pride along with a 50¢ piece from the Real Estate Man — in which event the running schedule of the system goes completely to pot.

One of the worst things the patrons of the trolley have to endure is when the Skipper takes the ash pan out of the car stove to put the ashes on the rails so that the car can make the grade at Goat Hill.

After being pestered for over a month about it the Skipper climbed up on the roof to fix a leak no bigger than your finger and just see what happened!

Oftimes the Skipper's wife finds it necessary to take the car away from him when his friends have been a bit too kind to him on New Years Day.

THE SKIPPER IS TOO GOOD
A FISHERMAN HIMSELF NOT TO
HOLD UP TRAFFIC FOR A FEW MINUTES
IN THIS SORT OF A SITUATION.

WHEN THE CAR IS ABOUT HALF FILLED
AND ALL PASSENGERS CROWD OVER BESIDE
THE CAR STOVE THE SKIPPER ALWAYS
REFUSES TO GO AHEAD UNTIL THEY
RIGHT THE OLD BOAT.

ED PENNY THE NEW TRAFFIC
OFFICER AT DEAD CENTER, NEVER
HAS LIKED THE SKIPPER OF THE
TROLLEY AND IS CERTAINLY MAKING
LIFE MISERABLE FOR HIM.

THE SALESMAN PRESENTED THE
SKIPPER WITH A CIGAR IN THE HOPE OF
HAVING HIM MAKE QUICKER TIME TO THE DEPOT
BUT IT PRODUCED JUST THE OPPOSITE EFFECT.

THE SKIPPER'S INTIMATE KNOWLEDGE OF MEN, WOMEN AND EVENTS IN THE DISTRICT MAKES IT POSSIBLE FOR HIM TO RENDER BOTH PUBLIC AND PERSONAL SERVICE ON OCCASIONS.

Bert Eggers is too big to get inside the car and sit in the middle so when Bert is the only passenger the Skipper has to run the car in a rather *unusual* manner.

ED WORTLE HAS BUILT HIMSELF A PLATFORM FROM WHICH HE CAN STEP RIGHT OFF ONTO THE ROOF BECAUSE BY THE TIME THE CAR REACHES HIS HOUSE EVERY MORNING THERE AIN'T ANY OTHER PLACE TO RIDE.

23

24

25

THAT CURVE, WHICH THE SKIPPER PUT IN THE TRACK FORTY YEARS AGO FOR THE CONVENIENCE OF PATRONS, HAS BECOME OF SOME USE AGAIN.

WHENEVER THE SKIPPER READS ABOUT THE RECONSTRUCTION FINANCE CORPORATION GRANTING SOME BIG LOAN.

ON COLD MORNINGS SLIM EVARTS USES HIS WIFE'S REDUCING CABINET TO KEEP WARM WHILE WAITING FOR THE CAR.

28

34

MICKEY McGUIRE MADE A HIGH DIVING CHAMPION OUT OF EDDIE SIMS (22)

THAT FAT BOY THAT MICKEY McGUIRE IS ALWAYS CHASING (16)

McGUIRE WILL BE MADE A MEMBER OF THE MOTHERS' AID SOCIETY YET (18)

A PRESENT FOR MICKEY (HIMSELF) McGUIRE (24)

OFFICER MILLER, ARCH ENEMY OF MICKEY (HIMSELF) McGUIRE, WAS STRUCK ON THE HEAD BY A PIECE OF FLYING DEBRIS THE DAY OF THE BIG WIND.

MICKEY McGUIRE OFTEN HAS A GALLERY TO WATCH THE SHOTS HE MAKES DELIVERING THE AFTERNOON PAPERS

WHEN MICKEY McGUIRE STEPS ON THE SCALES UP AT THE CORNER DRUG STORE

THE FAT BOY THAT MICKEY McGUIRE HAS BEEN "AFTER"

THE TERRIBLE TEMPERED MR. BANG & THE PAPER NAPKIN

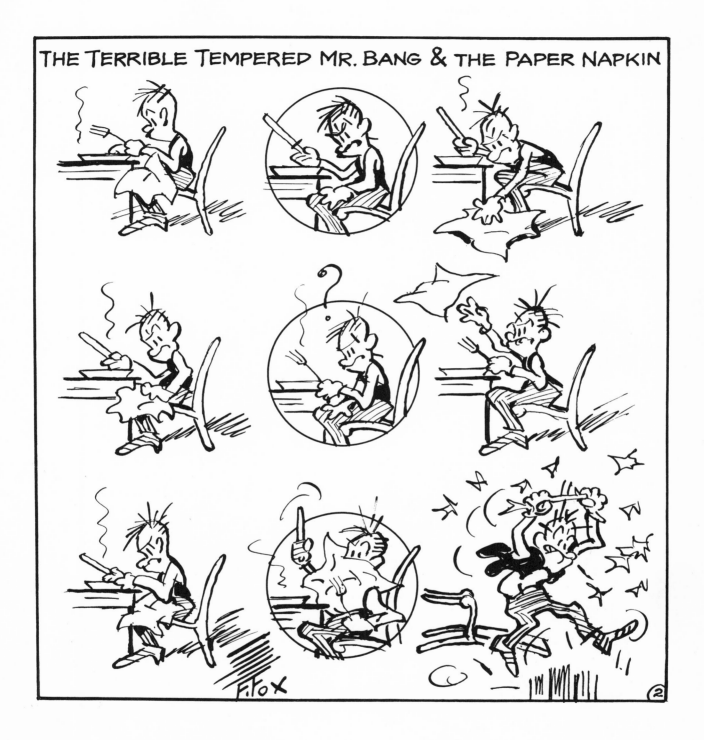

70

MOTHER WOULD PROBABLY HAVE THROWN A DUCK FIT IF SHE COULD HAVE SEEN KATRINKA AND THE BABY GOING OVER TO THE ICE PLANT FIRE.

SEVERAL PEOPLE GATHERED OUTSIDE THE WINDOW TO RUBBER AT HER AND ALL SHE WAS DOING WAS LOOKING AT SOME COLORED PICTURES IN THE DICTIONARY.

IT WILL BE MANY A DAY BEFORE MOTHER LETS HER PUT ANOTHER LETTER IN THE MAIL BOX WITHOUT LEAVING THE CAR.

KATRINKA!

"THAT BAG! THE POWERFUL KATRINKA CANT LIFT THAT BAG! WANTA BET A DOLLAR SHE CANT?

YEP!

"I DONT NOTICE HER LIFTING IT ANY

FIRE PLUG!

27

THE POWERFUL KATRINKA CAN AMUSE A CHILD IN MORE DIFFERENT WAYS!

THE POWERFUL KATRINKA

THE SWEAT BEES KEPT BOTHERING THE POWERFUL KATRINKA WHILE SHE WAS ROLLING THE LAWN

THE POWERFUL KATRINKA WAS ASKED TO BRING IN THE NEW TENNIS NET

The professor will never be able to fish successfully as long as he has any sort of a book with him.

By FONTAINE FOX.

84

THEY THOUGHT AUNT EPPIE HOGG COULD GET ABOUT ON THAT SORE FOOT IF SOMEONE MADE HER AN OVERSIZED, REINFORCED CRUTCH

"It just ain't no use! When I get it under my arm I CAN'T get it on the ground!"

TACTLESS TILLIE TOMPKINS PULLS ANOTHER ONE AT AUNT EPPIE HOGG'S TEA

"Who was it who asked me why I gave up playing the HARP?"

OF COURSE, AUNT EPPIE HOGG WAS NEVER TOLD ABOUT UNCLE BEN WORTLE'S MISTAKE

"No! No! Uncle Ben! The TABLE is in there!"

AUNT EPPIE HOGG SOMETIMES THINKS SHE'LL HAVE TO QUIT LENDING THE CHILDREN STOCKINGS TO HANG UP CHRISTMAS EVE

"Aunt Eppie sez please don't run through town with her stocking like that!"

Using a bucket of bran to lead the Cow onward, Tomboy Taylor carries out her threat to wreck the club-house after the members had black balled her just because she was a girl.

THREE MEMBERS WERE "KICKED OUT OF THE CLUB" LAST WEEK. MORE MEMBERS WOULD HAVE BEEN KICKED OUT IF MORE HAD BEEN IN IT WHEN TOMBOY TAYLOR'S GANG DESCENDED ON THE PLACE.

"THEY GOT IT FIXED UP PRETTY SLICK IN HERE"

"HERE'S YER OL' HATS"

"LES GIT A COP! THAT'S OUR CLUB."

E-DITH!

IT SEEMS AS THOUGH WHENEVER TOMBOY DECIDES TO PULL OFF ONE OF HER STUNTS (SUCH AS WALKING OUT TO THE END OF THE SPRING BOARD ON STILTS) THEN IS THE VERY TIME HER MOTHER WILL HAPPEN ALONG.

"YOOHOO! EDDIE! LOOK TH' SHIMMY!"

AW! I BETCHA COULDN'T DO IT IF THE ENGINE WUZN'T RUNNIN'

WHEN HER MOTHER LEFT THE FLIVVER, TOMBOY SEIZED THE OPPORTUNITY TO GIVE AN EXHIBITION OF MODERN DANCING.

Tomboy Taylor felt that if she jumped to the floor it would shake things down so that she could eat some more turkey.   *By Fontaine Fox.*

96

108

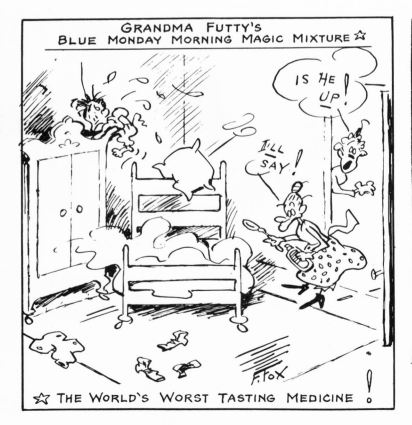

114

FUTTY BRINGS HOME A JUG OF RARE ~~CKER~~ ON A VERY SLIPPERY DAY

GRANPAW FUTTY HATES CITY FOLKS

JUST LIKE 'EM TO HOLD BACK WITH THEIR PRESENT-STYLE BATHING SUITS TILL MY EYESIGHT IS PRACTICALLY GONE!

~~LY~~ MORNING GAME IN THE PARK

~~MBER~~ NOW, IF ~~PAW~~ TOUCHES THE ~~NER~~ WITH HIS CANE THE PLAY IS STOPPED!

GRANDPAW FUTTY
HAS BEEN DINING OUT WITH HIS DAUGHTER IN THE BIG CITY

IT'S A CLAMP! TO KEEP THEM DURN WAITERS FROM WHISKING MY PLATE AWAY WHEN I'M ONLY HALF FINISHED!

120

124

WHEN THEY STOP AT YOUR PLACE, UNHOOK IT AND SEND IT BACK TO ME BEHIND SOME OTHER CAR

PLEASURE DRIVING

LEM WORTLE, THE PRACTICAL JOKER, IS AT IT AGAIN

"NO TIME TO GET SHOVELS! WE GOTTA DIG HIM OUT WITH OUR HANDS!"

LEM WORTLE, THE PRACTICAL JOKER, CAN WORK THIS ONE ONLY ON THOSE WHO ARE NOT ACQUAINTED WITH HIM

"HE SAID THE BODY WAS BATTERED ALMOST BEYOND RECOGNITION; IT WOULD MAKE ME SICK TO LOOK AT IT!"

128

"TEENY" TOMP
WORLD'S SMALLEST FOOTBALL PLAYER
ADDYAMEAN, – FUMBLE! 'TEENY' TOMPKINS
AS THAT BALL AND HE'S GOIN'
T' TOWN WITH IT!"
F. FOX
25

"TEENY" TOMPKINS, THE WORLD'S SMALLEST FOOTBALL PLAYER
"THEY ALWAYS PLACE-KICK 'TEENY' WHEN HE HOLDS THE BALL SO HE CAN FLIP IT OVER THE BAR IF IT'S SHORT!"
F. FOX

"TEENY" TOM
WORLD'S SMALLEST FOOTBALL PLAYER
"HE'S BLOCKED THE KICK!"
F. FOX
21

"TEENY" TOMPKINS, THE WORLD'S SMALLEST FOOTBALL PLAYER
4
"WOT D'YA MEAN, – 'HE STUMBLED OVER SOMPIN'? HE WUZ TACKLED BY 'TEENY' TOMPKINS!"
F. FOX

136

28

142

WHEN WILLIE'S AIRPLANE WAS ALL FINISHED IT WAS HIS MOTHER WHO CAME OVER AND MADE THE FIRST TAKE-OFF

"SHE TOOK OFF THEM NEW BABY CARRIAGE WHEELS HE HAD ON IT!"

MOTHER FINDS OUT WHY IT ALWAYS TAKES WILLIE SO MUCH LONGER TO BRING HOME A LOAF OF THAT FRENCH BREAD

"WILLIE! WHAT SORT OF LANGUAGE IS THAT! 'A SOCK ON THE PUSS'!"

WILLIE HAS SOLD SEVERAL OF HIS CANDID CAMERA SNAPSHOTS TO SISTER'S BEAU

"DID YOU HEAR THAT CLICK!"

"WILBERT!"

— IT'S NOT SUPPOSED TO BE LIT — IT'S FULLA CANDY!

"WILBERT!"

LITTLE STANLEY'S TOY TELEPHONE

" HE'S GOT ANOTHER 'WRONG NUMBER'! WATCH HIM GIVE AN IMITATION OF HIS FATHER!"

IF THAT FRISBIE GIRL TACKLES HIM AGAIN, LITTLE STANLEY IS DETERMINED TO BE IN BETTER SHAPE FOR THE FIGHT

" MOM, COULD I GO TO THE BARBER AND HAVE M' HAIR CUT SHORT? I MEAN REAL SHORT!"

By cutting some holes in an old hat box, Vernon McNutt made a phone booth so he could talk with more privacy to his sweetie over the <u>Boarding-House</u> phone

EVENT OF THE WEEK
Ezra Fairchild's daughter returned home from college and announced she was a Communist

Excitement At The Post Office
Banker Flint tries to keep 'em from picking up a Comic Valentine he'd crumpled and thrown away

The Big Wind blew enuf stuff over against the cliff on Hy Turkin's place to last 'em a lifetime

165

"THAT'S EDDIE WHOOZIS, HARVARD'S GREAT BLOCKING BACK!"

FARMER FENNEL HAS ADDED SOMETHING TO HIS ENJOYMENT OF THE GAME OF GOLF

ZEKE WINGFIELD'S OLDEST BOY IS RAISING CAIN ABOUT HAVING TO GO BACK TO SCHOOL AGAIN THIS YEAR

WILBERT THE WEEPER

THE SMITHS ARE MIGHTY PROUD OF THEIR NEW RUBBER-TIRED BALL-BEARING BABY CARRIAGE

"KNOBHEAD" NEWSOME, WHOSE WIFE IS TOONERVILLE'S BEST SHOT WITH A PLATE OR A TEA CUP

KIBBY (KIBITZER) SNOOP, WHO HAS STRAINED HIS NECK FOR 50 YEARS WATCHING OTHER PEOPLE PLAY GAMES

"SNIDE" SANDERS, THE FAMOUS GOAT-GETTER

173

NOT "MOTHERS' DAY" OR "FATHERS' DAY" BUT "GOOD FOR NOTHING UNCLES' DAY" IS THE BIG DAY, LOCALLY

GOOD FOR NOTHING UNCLES DAY

UNCLE JOE

UNCLE FELIX

OUR UNCLE BEN

ANNUAL PARADE

EVENT OF THE WEEK— THE SCRAP METAL PILE IN MONUMENT CIRCLE AT EAST SCURVEE WAS STRUCK BY LIGHTNING

FIND THE MAN WHOSE YOUNGSTER HAS GOT INTO THE CELLAR AND DRAGGED OUT MOST OF HIS "HOOCH" DISTILLING APPARATUS

He has been just about ready to give up the job ever since his wife hit on that idea of fastening the signals onto her churn handle.

POST OFFICE

STOP GO

CHURNING!

180

182
182